SERVANTHOOD

MISSIONS TRAINING

ENCOURAGING CHRISTIANS TO BE SERVANTS

STUDENT WORKBOOK

BY DON JEFFREYS

WestBow Press books may be ordered through booksellers or by contacting:

WestBow Press
A Division of Thomas Nelson & Zondervan
1663 Liberty Drive
Bloomington, IN 47403
www.westbowpress.com
1 (866) 928-1240

Scripture taken from the King James Version of the Bible.

Scripture quotations taken from The Holy Bible, New International Version® NIV® Copyright © 1973 1978 1984 2011 by Biblica, Inc. TM. Used by permission. All rights reserved worldwide.

ISBN: 978-1-9736-7161-9 (sc)
ISBN: 978-1-9736-7162-6 (e)

Library of Congress Control Number: 2019911353

Print information available on the last page.

WestBow Press rev. date: 6/30/2020

WESTBOW
PRESS®
A DIVISION OF THOMAS NELSON
& ZONDERVAN

Foreword

According to a 2018 study conducted by the Barna Group and the Seed Company (Translating the Great Commission), 51 percent of churchgoers do not know the term "Great Commission." This is a staggering number. The study was very revealing as well as troubling. A decline in Great Commission education within local churches over the last several decades has produced believers who have a limited understanding of biblical missions. Such a decline has also produced believers who do not understand the panoramic view of God's self-revelation from eternity past to eternity future as well as not understanding their place in God's redemptive story. We are now dealing with, and have dealt with in the recent past, the results of a lack of proper biblical teaching on the Great Commission. There are specific examples of such Great Commission education taking place, but it is rather isolated while the majority of churches do not emphasize or provide such basic biblical discipleship. Such a reality is evidenced in the findings of the 2018 study.

As our churches engage with an ever-changing culture, we need practical training manuals, which assist us to meet the challenges we face. Servanthood seeks to reverse the downward spiral of biblical ignorance and preparedness our churches are experiencing. The materials you are about to study will assist you and you church as active participants in Christ's command to make disciples of all people groups. Servanthood is a practical training manual. Its goal is to aid any individual, congregation or organization to get to the next level in Gospel advancement. Servanthood will refocus you, from your current level of Gospel engagement to where you should be. You are about to study a planned approach, which covers a wide variety of preparation topics.

Don Jeffreys is a trusted minister of the Gospel with many years of faithful service. Servanthood is the result of Don taking on a new challenge as Mission Pastor and not finding specific training materials. What Don has prepared is a well thought out manual with great advice and information. Any individual, church or organization will benefit from this tremendous resource.

Darrell Horn, D. Min.

Executive Director

San Antonio Baptist Association

My Story

After 50+ years in full-time ministry, I felt the Lord directing me to retire from the pastorate. For years, thinking about this day, I was praying for a place do missions and senior adult work. The day after announcing my resignation, I met up with a dear friend, Pastor Ray Brown. We had known each other, and I had been in the right place at the right time to help him and his church years earlier. We had become good friends, working together in various ministries.

We had not seen each other for a while. He asked about me, and I told him I had just retired. He asked me to make an appointment with his secretary. There he said, "You know, we have a few Anglos in our church." "Yes," I said, "and some other races also." He said, "I want to integrate my church more, but I know I can't do that until I integrate my staff. I believe you have some years left. What would you like to do?"

I thought, "Wow! No one ever asked me what I would like to do in the ministry!" I told him about praying for a place to do missions and senior adult work, but I had no idea where. Most churches raise leaders up from within.

He said, "I don't have a leader for either one. Come on over." So, the next day after I gave in to the Lord, He answered my prayers. Now I am serving on the greatest staff I could have dreamed, being part of Resurrection Church, with two locations, Schertz and San Antonio.

Later, I admitted to my pastor that, as I prayed for a place to serve, the only church that came to mind was Resurrection. But I never thought it was possible, so I never pursued it. Pastor Brown also admitted to me that as he prayed about integrating his staff, he thought about me. But he too, never followed up and the day we met outside Schertz City Hall; he had not planned on inviting me to join his staff. What a joy that we can see the Lord's footprint as we look back!

I came to Resurrection March 27, 2012. The first Sunday I was invited to preach and be introduced. I asked, "How many were involved in a mission experience last year? With approximately 1200 in attendance in two services, a scattering few raised their hands. We issued the challenge for everyone to go on at least one mission experience. Seven years later, after four of these trainings, we now have more than 1,000 members on at least one mission experience a year. The church has been blessed! We are baptizing over 100 new believers a year; the Kingdom of heaven is expanding locally and beyond. We now have four services each Sunday with a membership of over 5,000 and we believe there are greater things ahead.

What I share in this manual is not from years of experience, but from my first seven years at Resurrection and from the research of others with far more experience. Yet, when I started preparing to train my teams for servanthood, I didn't find a manual or comprehensive instruction anywhere. There is more material available now, but at the time, I didn't find it.

This instruction has received great reviews, some of which you will see in the Foreword and the introductory letter from Pastor Brown, as well as in the following text. It is my prayer that it may be used to help train others who will answer the Lord's call to go and serve, for a day, a week or two, or for the rest of your life. As so many have expressed: The Lord has blessings in store which you will never experience until you go and serve.

The Lord's Call

Servanthood centers on the Great Commandment, Great Commission, Great Promise, and Great Assignment

The Great Commandment: Jesus replied: "'Love the Lord your God with all your <u>heart</u> and with all your <u>soul</u> and with all your <u>mind</u>.' This is the first and greatest commandment. And the second is like it: 'Love your neighbor as yourself.'" Matthew 22:37-39 (NIV)

The Great Commission: Jesus came to them and said, "All authority in heaven and on earth has been given to me. Therefore, go and <u>make disciples</u> of all nations, <u>baptizing them</u> in the name of the Father and of the Son and of the Holy Spirit, and <u>teaching them</u> to obey everything I have commanded you. And surely, I am with you always, to the very end of the age." Matthew 28:18-20 (NIV)

The Great Promise: Jesus said, "But ye shall receive power, after that the Holy Ghost is come upon you: and ye shall be witnesses unto me both in Jerusalem, and in all Judaea, and in Samaria, and unto the uttermost part of the earth" (Acts 1:8 KJV)

The Great Assignment: ye shall be witnesses unto me both in Jerusalem, and in all Judaea, and in Samaria, and unto the uttermost part of the earth

Jerusalem – _____

Judea – _____

Samaria – _____

World – _____

Take the Command, Commission, Promise and Assignment _____and _____

Personally means – I must believe this is meant for me and our church.
Seriously means – I must get serious about what the Lord has told me/us to do.

Evaluation Question: What was the most beneficial (new or best reminders)?
Answer: The translation of the Great Assignment stood out to me.

—Cynthia Gibbs
2017 Mission Training

Disciples

Our desire is to go and make disciples. At the same time, become better, growing disciples ourselves.

Make Disciples

Always remember that Jesus commanded us to go and _____, not just to do good humanitarian deeds, not even just to make converts. We want to build relationships, not just "win 'em and drop 'em." But remember as someone has so accurately said, "We haven't made a disciple until the person you led to the Lord is making disciples."

Become Better, Growing Disciples

While working to make disciples of others, we ourselves are always in a constant state of _____ in the Lord. Our desire is to put more missionaries on the field. But we recognize that not everyone is ready for an overseas mission trip. Some need to start at home. Others are ready to grow and go on a trip to work and minister outside of home, yet not yet on the foreign field.

We challenge our people to go on a mission trip in _____ of the four areas of our Lord's commission. Our assignment is not Jerusalem or Judea or Samaria or the world, but Jerusalem and Judea and Samaria and the world. Yet not everyone is on the same plane in their missional vision, confidence or maturity. We are not all ready to go off, but we can all serve – somewhere, in some way, to make a difference in someone's life for the Lord.

Missions Ministry God's Hands

Invariably, when we ask what church members understand of missions, they reply with something like "going overseas" or "giving to our foreign missions offering." Very few really get the concept that Servanthood to the people we live and work around and throughout our state, nation, and world is all part of our responsibility as servants of our Lord Jesus. All of this is part of our commission.

The diagram on the right show the ministries we call Servanthood or Missions and with these ministries we try to attack our assignment in the four areas of the Great Commission.

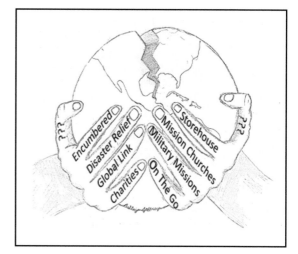

LAB WORK

(Suggestions in Leader's Guide)

Evaluation Question: Overall what did we do well? I thought the information sharing was very good. Having people participate in Labs was very important.

—Chris Evans
2017 Mission Training

Evaluation Question: What can we do to improve – answer: Practice, Practice, Practice and stay in prayer.

—Oletia Bethea
2014 Mission Trip to Haiti

Evaluation Question: What was the most beneficial (new or best reminders) you received? Answer: I enjoyed the moment when we were asked to share the Gospel with partners

—Gregorio A. Armand
2017 Mission Training

Evaluation Question: What did we do well?
Answer: Sharing past experiences. Lab work

—Terry Hughes
2017 Mission Training

Evaluation Question: What was the most beneficial (new or best reminders) you received? Answer: I liked the personal practice…I need more practice witnessing.

—Gennelle Conway
2017 Mission Training

I looked for things that I can do when I return, like staying in touch, and doing personal things to show the love of Christ.

—Sheron Green
2014 Mission Trip to Belize

Evaluation Question: What did we do well?
Answer: providing the booklet/guide to this training. It was helpful in the classroom and to review as we prepare for missions

—Lourita Schafer
2017 Mission Training

<u>HOMEWORK</u>

Homework for each session is the same
Earmark this page so you can refer back to it after each session

Review the Introduction – what were some of the highlights you want to remember?
Read Next Session (Pencil in answers you anticipate)
Bring to Class Next Session:
    Bible and Pen
    Personal Calendar
    I-phone or Android with downloaded 1Cross app
    Humble Spirit

Devotional and Prayer

Getting Ready By
UNDERSTANDING

Understand our Mission

1. **Remember our overall** _____

Never stray from your church vision/mission statement – this is who and what we are!

2. **Be a Team**

T = _____: We are a team! Pitch in, help, don't wait for others. Go the extra mile.
E = _____: Encourage teammates. Keep your words positive. Build others up.
A = _____: Watch your attitude – especially in tough times.
M = _____: Mission is #1. Your needs and desires must take a back seat to the mission.

Commit to this ideal: For the duration of this trip I will submit to my mission, team and leaders.

> Make every missionary feel like they are part of the mission. BE A TEAM.
>
> —Sheron Green
> 2014 Mission Trip to Belize

3. **Plan for an End Result –** _____

4. **Know your purpose –** _____

Why are you going? What do you hope and plan to accomplish?

> Evaluation Question: How effective do you feel your team was in accomplishing your mission?
> Answer: Very effective, the Word was shared and projects completed. Evening debriefs were necessary and helpful.
>
> —Don Young
> 2014 Mission Trip to Haiti

> Mission trips are very important. I really feel that we need to realize this is not a vacation, but a working mission trip. That it is not about us. We are the body of Christ, and we all have a part to do. We much decrease so that Jesus can increase. That should be expressed in our training.
>
> —Sheron Green
> 2014 Mission Trip to Belize

Understand our Witness

Why do we Go?

1. **We go to** _____! Look for opportunities to witness – everywhere, every day!

We do not go just to do good humanitarian work, but to share the gospel!

2. **We go to** _____!

    We must leave such a good reputation and report that:

    a. We are invited back.

    b. Our host will have open doors to minister when we leave.

Do not underestimate this critical part of our mission purpose.

Debrief at first Haiti trip, 2012

3. **We go to** _____

4. **We do not go to** _____!

Most important, please do not go on a mission trip expecting anything but to work and work hard, witness and witness faithfully, serve and serve loyally, sacrifice and sacrifice willingly and uncomfortably!

(Stearns, <u>The Hole In Our Gospel</u>, p. 302)

Who Can Go?

A. **Your team leader should have** _____ **for answering this question**

B. _____ **can go!**

Where do we Go? _____!

James 2:5: Listen, my dear brothers and sisters: Has not God chosen those who are poor in the eyes of the world to be rich in faith and to inherit the kingdom he promised those who love him?

James 2:6: But you have dishonored the poor. Is it not the rich who are exploiting you? Are they not the ones who are dragging you into court?

But the fact, is the _____are the neediest of the needy!

What do we go to Proclaim? Know _____so you will be able to share it!

A – _____your _____!

B – _____in the _____!

C – _____that Jesus is now your _____!

Carrefour, Haiti, 2012

When does our Witness Matter?

1. **Among our own team members –** _____!

John 13:35: By this everyone will know that you are my disciples, if you love one another."

Romans 12:10 Be devoted to one another in love. Honor one another above yourselves.

1 Thessalonians 4:9 Now about your love for one another we do not need to write to you, for you yourselves have been taught by God to love each other.

2. **Our (host organization and its leaders)** _____!

Hebrews 13:17: Have confidence in your leaders and submit to their authority, because they keep watch over you as those who must give an account. Do this so that their work will be a joy, not a burden, for that would be of no benefit to you.

3. **Our host nation –** _____!

1 Peter 2:13-14: Submit yourselves for the Lord's sake to every human authority: whether to the emperor, as the supreme authority, 14 or to governors, who are sent by him to punish those who do wrong and to commend those who do right.

4. **Our Witness Plans**

A. _____— Download App and practice

B. _____– Practice using tracts everywhere

C. _____

The tools for sharing the Gospel were very good!

Dominican Republic, 2017

—Chris Evans
2017 Mission Training

Evaluation Question: What was the most beneficial (new or best reminders)?
Answer: I loved the example of the "Bridge" an easy personal tract.

—Lolly Faison
2017 Mission Training

Understand our Expectations

Expect _____ *Which most organizations now require*

Know the _____ *Which you are usually expected to raise*

Take along some extra _____ *Which for souvenirs, possibly travel, etc.*

Be Prepared for _____

Get Your _____

Get into the Culture:

Again, we remind you to _____ for the experience

It is imperative for _____ be familiar with the cultural values

Go to the _____ **or** _____ and look up the place you will serve, the specific area if possible

Spend Time with the _____

Family home on Belo Mountain, Haiti

1. Remember we are going to minister to and serve _____.
2. Think about your _____
3. Be _____
4. Be _____

Be _____

Resurrection Ministries with Haitians on Belo Mountain, Haiti, 2014

Be Faithful to all _____

These training sessions will not be the only meetings you will be expected to attend. As you focus in on your particular trip, specific training and team meeting relating to that trip will be required.

Team meeting before trip, Belize, 2014

Understand our Commitment

LAB WORK

(Suggestions in Leader's Guide)

HOMEWORK
(See page 3)

Devotional and Prayer

Getting Ready
PERSONALLY

Personal _____ – Dates, Plan of approach

Place your calendar in a prominent place where you will necessarily look at it every day to be reminded.

Personal _____ – Acquiring Passport/Visa, Three Copies

What is the difference between a passport and a visa? Passports are for _____trips outside the United States. Visas are for _____stays, usually more than thirty days.

To get a passport, go to your nearest Post Office. Plan at least six months out (earlier is even better).

YOUR PASSPORT NEEDS TO BE VALID FOR AT LEAST _____AFTER YOUR RETURN.

Make _____of your passport! Your Leader will tell you what to do with them.

If your passport is damaged, waterlogged, lost or stolen, you will not be able to get back on the airplane to get home until it is replaced. You will need to go to an American Embassy in the country where you are and apply for a replacement and having a copy of your old one will expedite the process.

Personal Comfort

Our _____

Tap Tap community transportation, Haiti

1. We may travel in rough vehicles or over rough terrain. Be prepared!

2. Walking may be necessary – a lot of walking!

3. Spend time _____and walking before leaving.

Our _____

Get a health _____   **Start** _____   **Keep** _____

Five Guidelines about _____— follow strictly the guidelines of your leader!

1. Do not _____ the water, nor any other liquid, unless you check with team leader and/or host

2. _____ safe drinking water

3. Do not _____ in water or hydrant

4. Do not eat _____ fruits or vegetables

5. Do not eat _____ unless approved

Hogs in village, Honduras

Know the _____

In many places, folks **get only** _____ **or** _____ **meals/day**

Take _____ for between meals.

Honduras, 2011

Special precautions:

1. **Never eat in the** _____ **of natives who do not get an extra meal each day.**

2. Similarly, when _____ is a premium, **never ask a native to get you a drink.** Remember that they are limited in the amount of water they may get to drink each day.

3. **Avoid** _____, _____ **any fresh** _____ **(uncooked),** _____ **foods, uncooked** _____, **fruit not** _____, **food from** _____.

4. **Reminder to drink only water** _____ **or** _____ **or** _____ **by our hosts**

5. Soft drinks are generally OK also, unless warned against them by your host.

But What If You Become _____ **or** _____

1. **Your team leader should be able to explain what procedures are in place.**

2. _____– On any given day, if you wake up feeling _____ or a little _____, or with even a little diarrhea — _____ **your team leader.**

Evaluation Question: What was the most beneficial (new or best reminders)?
Answer: Very informative about things we need to do to get ready for mission work: have passport, plan, take care of your health.

—Clisher Harmon
2017 Mission Training

Our _____

Most of the time we are given an agreement to sign or instructions to follow provided by our host.

In addition, we have our own Trip Agreement Form. We go over it in our _____(Appendix 2)

Our _____

We always want to represent our _____and our _____through our clothing! Please be aware –

1. No _____ads

2. No _____attention getters

3. No _____attire!

4. No _____attire!

Personal Sacrifice

Leave at Home:

Do Not Bring _____ – ($20's, 50's, and 100's).

Do Not Bring Expensive _____

Leave your _____ **at home!**

Leave a complete _____ **with a friend or family member back home**

Turn in the name and email address of _____ **contact person to your team leader**

Do Not Bring Anything you would _____

Do not bring or wear _____ **or** _____ **clothing**

Avoid Wearing _____

We recommend that you do not bring _____ **equipment**

By all means, leave the _____ **at home!**

Personal Practice

LAB WORK

(Suggestions in Leader's Guide)
HOMEWORK
(See page 3)

Devotional and Prayer

Getting Ready
SPIRITUALLY

Spiritual Accountability

Keep up with your _____

Your **devotional time** is primary for life as a Christian as well as for mission work.

Nothing is more important than your _____ with Christ.

Journal:

1. Even if you don't keep a personal diary, there will be _____ you will want to remember.

2. Be ready to_____to family, prayer partners and others. Journaling helps.

3. Also be prepared because you may be asked to give _____ to other groups.

Spiritual Praying

_____are critical to our success

Prayer is a vital _____ of all of our mission trips.

Prayer partners are part of our _____even though they don't make the trip with us.

You may have many prayer partners, but we ask that you turn in the names of two.

Before you fill out the prayer partner page, don't assume – ask the person if he/she is willing to serve and let them know that you need serious prayer partners.

Pray together _____ and pray _____

1. _____ in Your Prayer and Devotional Time.

2. _____ in Your Team Meetings.

Get serious about praying about your Lord's assignment and those assigned to go out with you!

3. _____ in special times of Prayer and Fasting.

Some service ministries recommend fasting and prayer at regular, weekly times. We recommend a prayer and fasting retreat before you leave.

> I will never forget what Bro. Don taught us about how to study the Bible during our prayer and fasting. It will stay with me forever.
> —Priscilla Armstrong
> 2014 Mission Trip to Haiti

Disaster Relief, Moore, OK., 2013

Belize Team Mtg., 2014

4. _____ while on the Field.

5. Teams are encouraged to pray and prepare together _____ while you are on the field.

6. We recommend your team pray **at least once** _____.

Ideas for Remembering Your Prayer Partners:

1. _____ **you go** set regular prayer times with prayer partners.

> Evaluation Question: What did we do well? Answer: …having prayer partners to come fast with us
>
> —Steve Bethea
> 2014 Mission Trip to Haiti

2. _____ **you go** remember to pray for them. Call or drop them a card soon after arriving. A souvenir card reminds them.

3. **When you** _____ remember to bring them back some trinket or souvenir, a "thank you" for their prayers, and a report of work and needs where served.

Ask _____ to pray

Medical Team praying with client, Honduras, 2011

Spiritual Assessment

Team Debrief Haiti, 2012

At the end of the trip – _____

I like to take **the last day of a trip to relax, debrief** and share together before returning.

Spiritual Ethics

Do not _____!

There is a real temptation to promise something when you encounter poverty.

Bring _____, Not _____

1. Due to customs regulations and because most hosts desire focus on_____-based ministry, most countries do not accept gifts-in-kind.

2. Four Reasons Why Not – Remember the Four C's:

    a. Creates _____— We have to decide whether we are helping or enabling.

    b. Causes _____— It may be hard for us to grasp how people, get so jealous.

    c. Cost of _____— The cost of customs is almost always exorbitantly expensive..

    d. Culminates in _____— Are we being honest?

    _____giving any monetary or other gifts, our leaders will check with our hosts.

We must remember that one of our goals is to assist our missionaries. If our hosts agree for us to bring gifts, they must be allowed to distribute them after we leave, not while we are there.

Spiritual Commitment

LAB WORK

(Suggestions in Leader's Guide)

HOMEWORK
(See page 3)

Devotional and Prayer

Getting Ready
EMOTIONALLY

Preparing for the _____ Experience

Learn the Culture

1. **Many times, there is a** _____
2. **Learn the** _____ **Use** _____.
3. **Show respect even if you** _____
4. **Prepare yourself for a** _____**experience**

Focus on _____Over _____

1. **Understanding others culture means understanding what** _____

2. **Put** _____**and** _____**above** _____**or** _____

Quit work to talk with people!

Evaluation Question: What was your best experience: Interacting with some of the children that I saw last year. It was rewarding to see some of the young men and they remembered our interaction.
— Don Young
2014 Mission Trip to Haiti

Linda Mills delivering love gifts to Schertz Fire Dept.

3. **Be satisfied with** _____

The needs are so great that any little thing we do will be an improvement and we can never do enough.
—Erskine Sealy
2014 Mission Trip to Haiti

Sitting with Honduran child, 2011

4. **Remember you are part of the** _____!

Your part is important, necessary. The puzzle is not be complete without you.
But you are not the _____nor_____piece.

Engage people. Use _____to organize their people.
Special Note, If we come and do not learn something, we have missed our mission!

Preparing for the_____Event

Elizabeth Elliott, whose first husband was killed in 1956 by Auca Indians in Ecuador (at the time unreached people group) said, "There is no faith without awareness of danger."

What can possibly go wrong?

Be ready

To_____   For _____

To _____   For _____

For _____   To _____ your very life

Voodoo Flag, Haiti

Security – Guidelines for safety to keep in mind while on a servanthood trip

Two Philosophies: Leaders or group must decide which to follow.

Haiti Team Shirts, 2013

1. _____

2. _____

Stay in _____– Never go off alone, there is safety in numbers.

Lock valuables _____

Be _____ of surroundings.

Never bring _____ into living area!

Blending with people, Haiti, 2013

Evaluation Question: What was the most beneficial (new or best reminders)?
Answer: Security warnings are important – good! The security video was very informative.
—Madeleine Roberts
2017 Mission Training

Three crucial points to remember:

1. Our _____

2. What if the _____had that philosophy

3. The safest place to be is _____

Prepare for _____Victory

Go _____submitting, but _____, with _____in the Lord

Go to _____and _____

> — We are going not just to do good humanitarian work
> — We are going to look for someone to share a_____
> — Keep your head up – Get in on what God's Doing

Remember stop the work — to _____, minister

— or to _____

— or _____ someone

Pic's with Joe Tex Band,
Lake Providence, LA, 2012

Be _____

Final Challenge

Let's Get In On What God Is Doing...

A. This means change our thinking From _____To _____

B. This means change our thinking From _____To _____

C. This means change our thinking From _____To _____

D. This means change our thinking From _____To _____

E. This means change our thinking From _____To _____

F. This means change our thinking From _____To _____

Have a good Experience!

What are the most important things you learned from these training sessions?

_____

_____

_____

Come Back Home To _____

Final LAB

I looked for things that I can do when I return, like staying in touch, and doing personal things to show the love of Christ.

—Sheron Green
2014 Mission Trip to Belize

Evaluation Question: What did we do well?
Answer: providing the booklet/guide to this training. It was helpful in the classroom and to review as we prepare for missions

.—Lourita Schafer
2017 Mission Training

Evaluation Question: What can we do to improve?
Answer: Keep doing the trips and we learn from experience what to do and what not to do

—Karen Minor-Hudson
2014 Mission Trip to Haiti

Thank you for the opportunity to participate. It was a life-changing trip and I think about what I learned almost daily. I have a renewed appreciation for what I have spiritually and materially.

—Bettina McGriggler
2014 Mission Trip to Belize

You should be given an evaluation form by your trainer
Please help us by taking a few moments to fill it out

And Remember:
Review Your Manual Periodically

Appendix 1: Training Material Resources Come From the Following Contributors

Baptist General Convention of Texas Disaster Relief
Ben Freeman, Retired, Texas Baptist Men Disaster Relief
Bill Bright, Crusade For Christ
Cooperative Baptist Fellowship
Ed Sundman, lay mission leader, First Baptist Church, Universal City, Texas
Ernie Rice, We Care Haiti
Every Nation Ministries
Four Corners International Ministries
Marla Bearden, Baptist General Convention of Texas Disaster Recovery
Mercy International Ministries, Albuquerque, New Mexico
On Mission Magazine
Paul Powell, The Last Word, Copyright 2004 Paul W. Powell
Resurrection Baptist Church Next Step 401
Rick Warren, Saddleback Church, Huntington Beach, California
Southern Baptist Convention
Texas Baptist Men Disaster Relief
The Hole In Our Gospel, by Richard Stearns, 2009-2010 World Vision, Inc., Thomas Nelson Publ.
Timothy Phanner, lay leader, Vista Community Church, Temple, Texas
Together for Hope, Lake Providence, LA
Trinity Baptist Church, San Antonio, Texas

I want to thank and give acknowledgement to each and every one who has had a part in my training and education to become a servant. I have learned from you, even when it did not always look like it at the time. Your input and influence in my life and ministry is more valuable than I can possibly put into words.

Don Jeffreys

Appendix 2: RESURRECTION'S Trip Agreement

I ACCEPT THE FOLLOWING GUIDELINES FOR MINISTRY, TEAMWORK, AND SAFETY AS WE SERVE:

1. I understand that I am a guest, working at the invitation of a local missionary or pastor and that the people, pastor and missionaries will stay long after I leave.

2. I understand that I have come to learn and work alongside of people God loves in the community where I will be serving. I will strive to remember not to be exclusive in my relationships. If a sweetheart, spouse or my child is on the trip, I will make every effort to interact with all members of the team and those we work with, not just my family or best friends.

3. I understand that I may come across procedures that I may feel are inefficient or attitudes that I might find closed-minded. I will resist the temptation to inform our hosts about "how I do things." I will be open to learning other people's methods and ideas. I will respect the hosts knowledge, insights, and instructions.

4. I understand that part of the purpose of this trip is to witness and experience faith lived out in a different setting from what I am accustomed to. I will respect and show gratitude for the host's view of Christianity.

5. I understand that I am expected to maintain a servant's attitude toward all nationals, locals and my teammates.

6. I understand I must watch my speech and not gossip or slander anyone.

7. I understand that the work may become tiring or at times seem boring, but I will refrain from complaining. I know travel can present numerous and unexpected and undesired situations, but the rewards of conquering the circumstances are immeasurable. I will strive to be creative and supportive.

8. I understand political situations may be tense at any given time. I will refrain from negative political comments or hostile discussions.

9. I understand I must be mature and I will refrain from any activity that could be construed as a romantic interest toward a national or local citizen. I realize that many activities that may seem innocent in our culture may seem inappropriate to others.

10. I understand that my witness and lifestyle is the most important thing I bring. I will abstain from the consumption of alcoholic beverages and the use of tobacco or illegal drugs while on the trip.

Signature:_____

Date:_____

Please attach a copy of your passport to be kept on file in case of emergency

Passport Number_____ Date of Expiration of Passport_____

Printed in the United States
By Bookmasters